LEARN TO READ
WITH IMAGES

Reading Made Easy With
MY FRIEND & ME

By Barnaby Pollock

First paperback edition December 2022

Text and Illustrations Copyright © 2022 Barnaby Pollock

ISBN 9798370099113 (Paperback)

LearnWithImages@Outlook.com

I'd like

I'd like

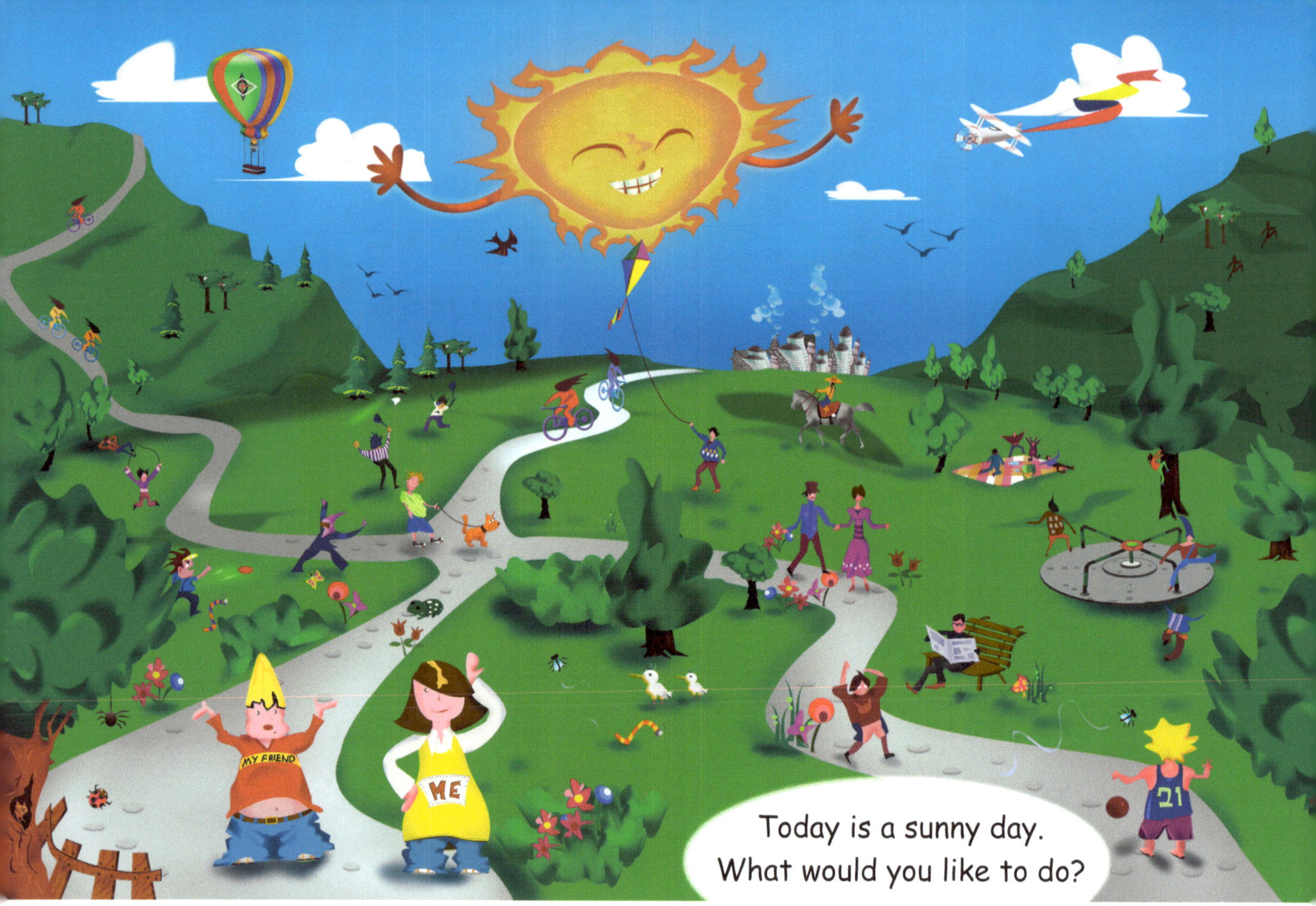

Today is a sunny day.
What would you like to do?

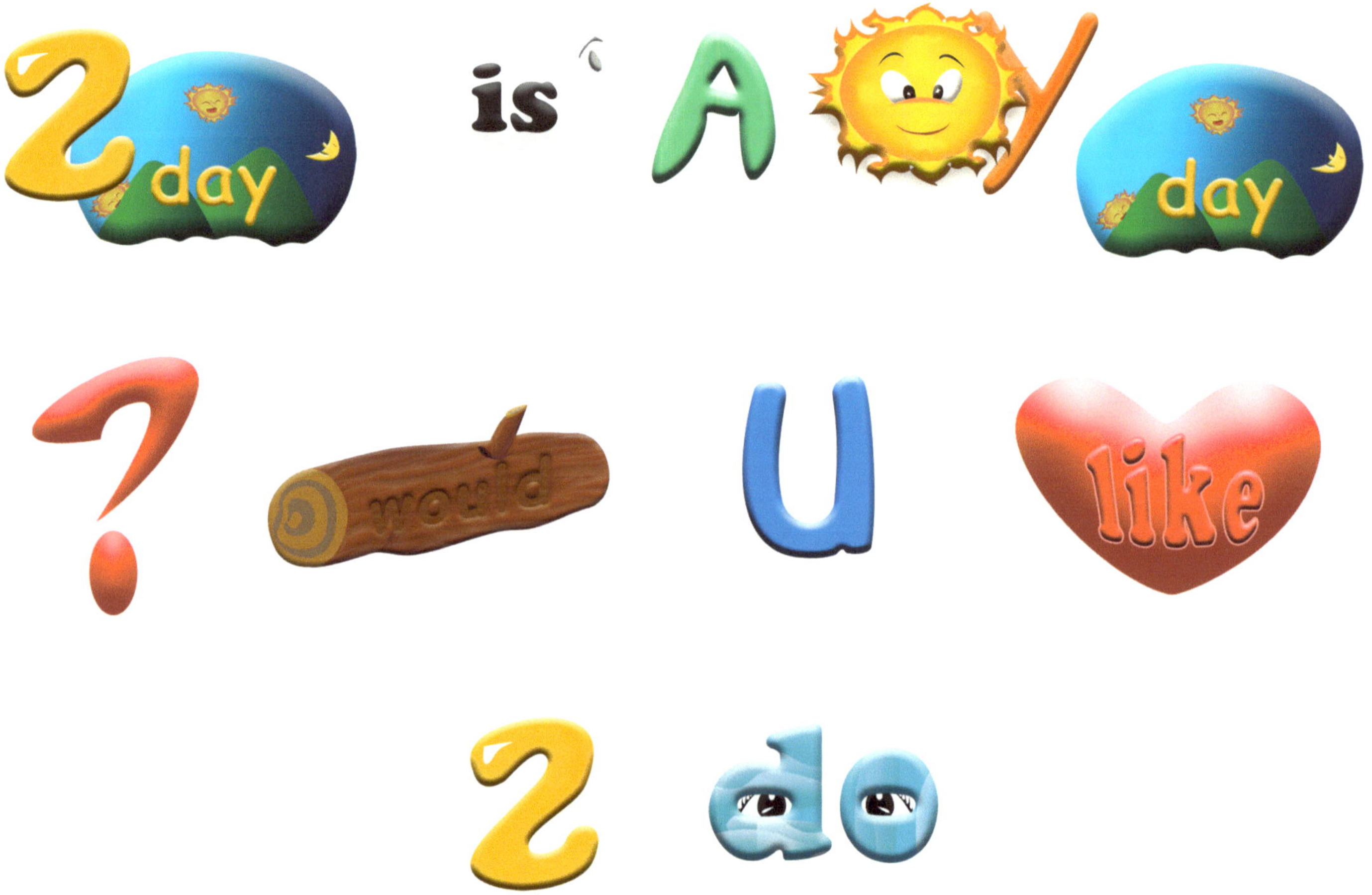

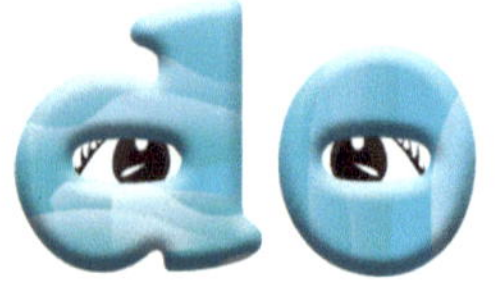

ME
MY FRIEND
ME
I'd like to slide
down the world's longest slide.
'd
like
2
the
's
est

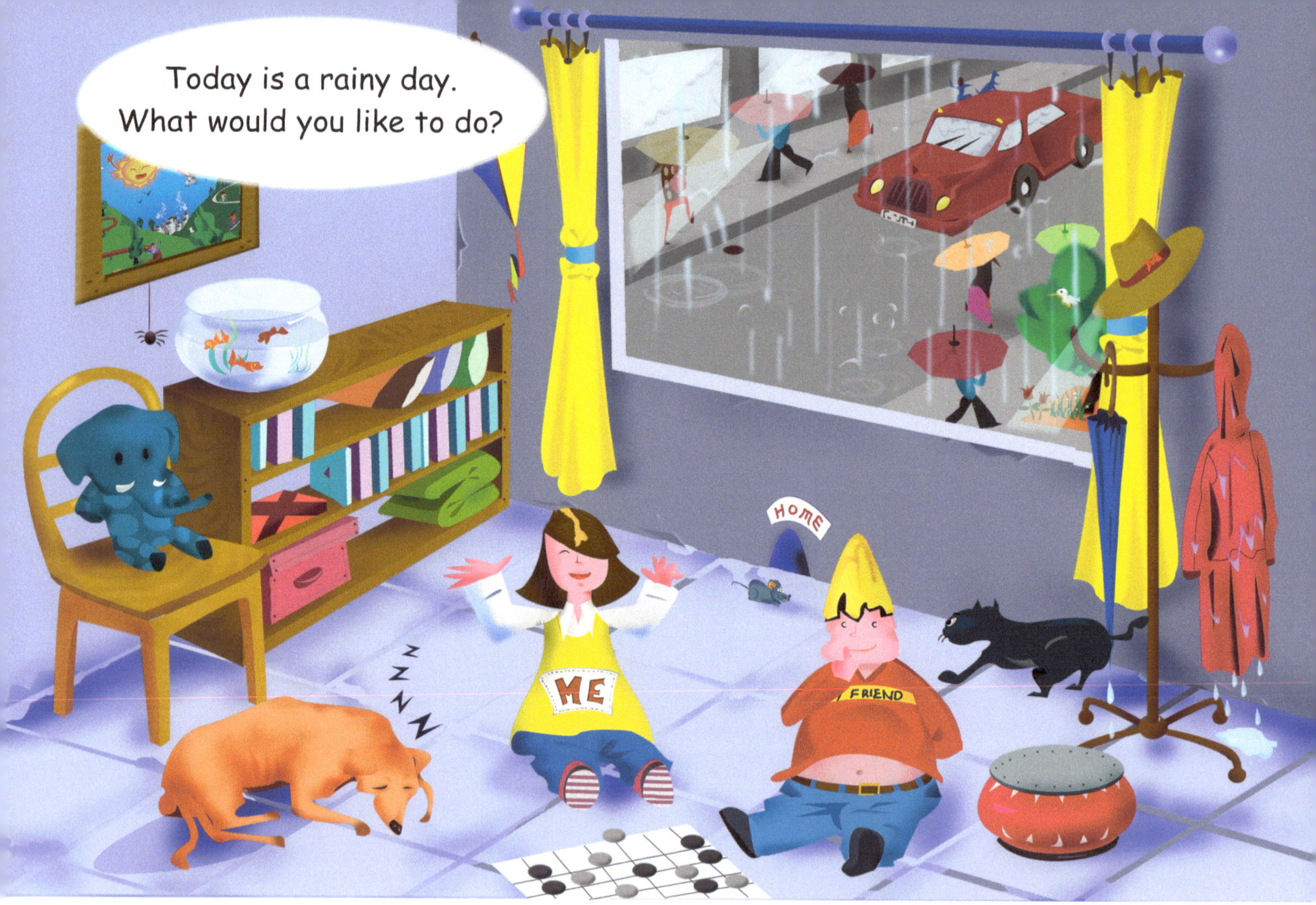

Today is a rainy day.
What would you like to do?

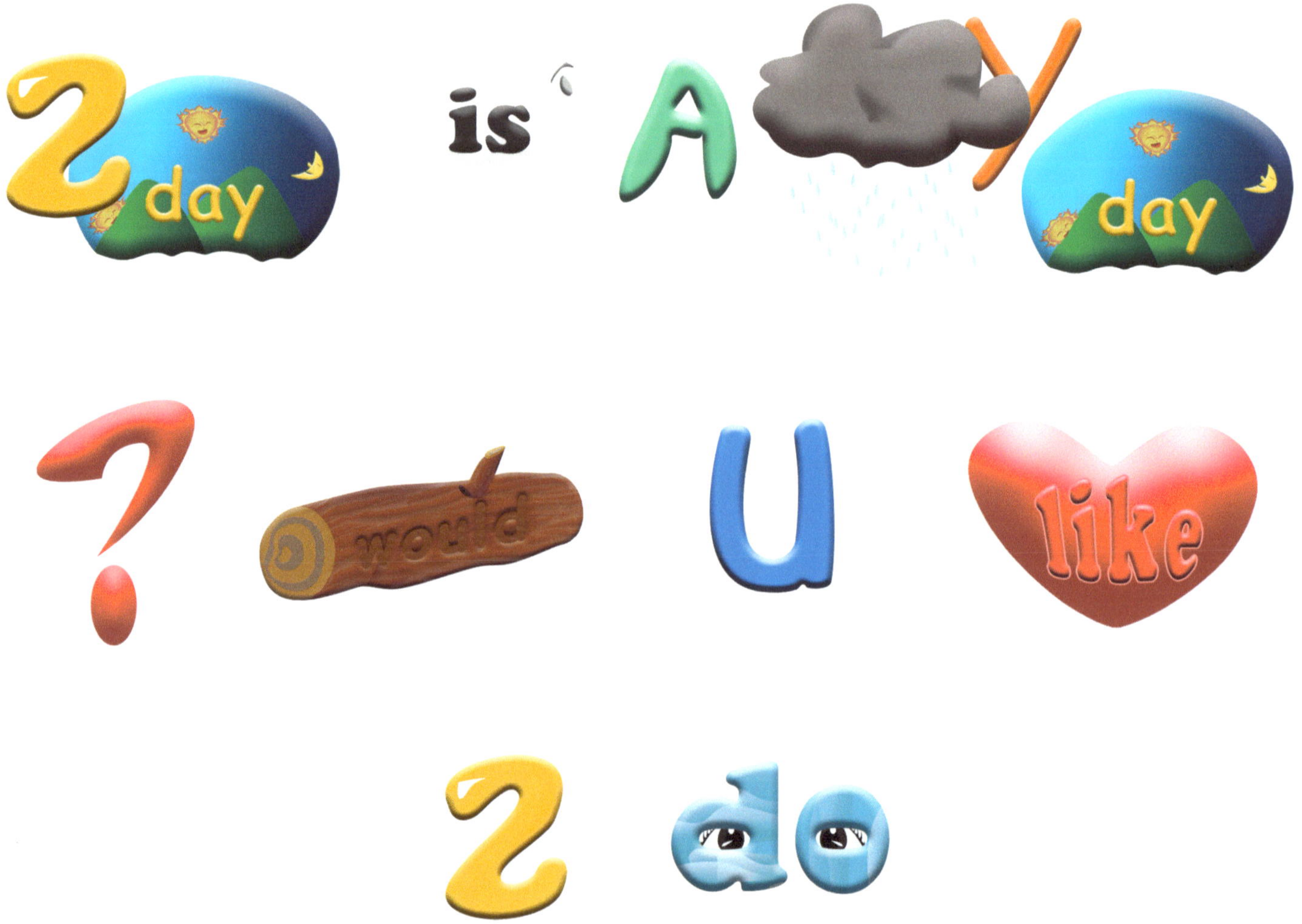

would

like

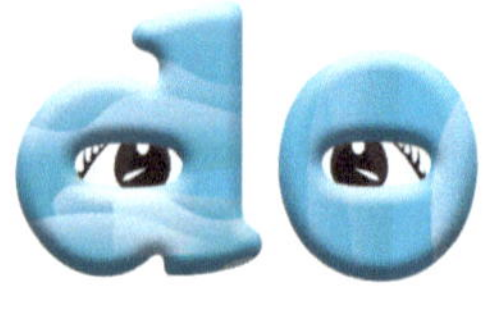
do

MY FRIEND
ME
I'd like to make
the world's coolest playhouse.
'd
like
2
the
's
est

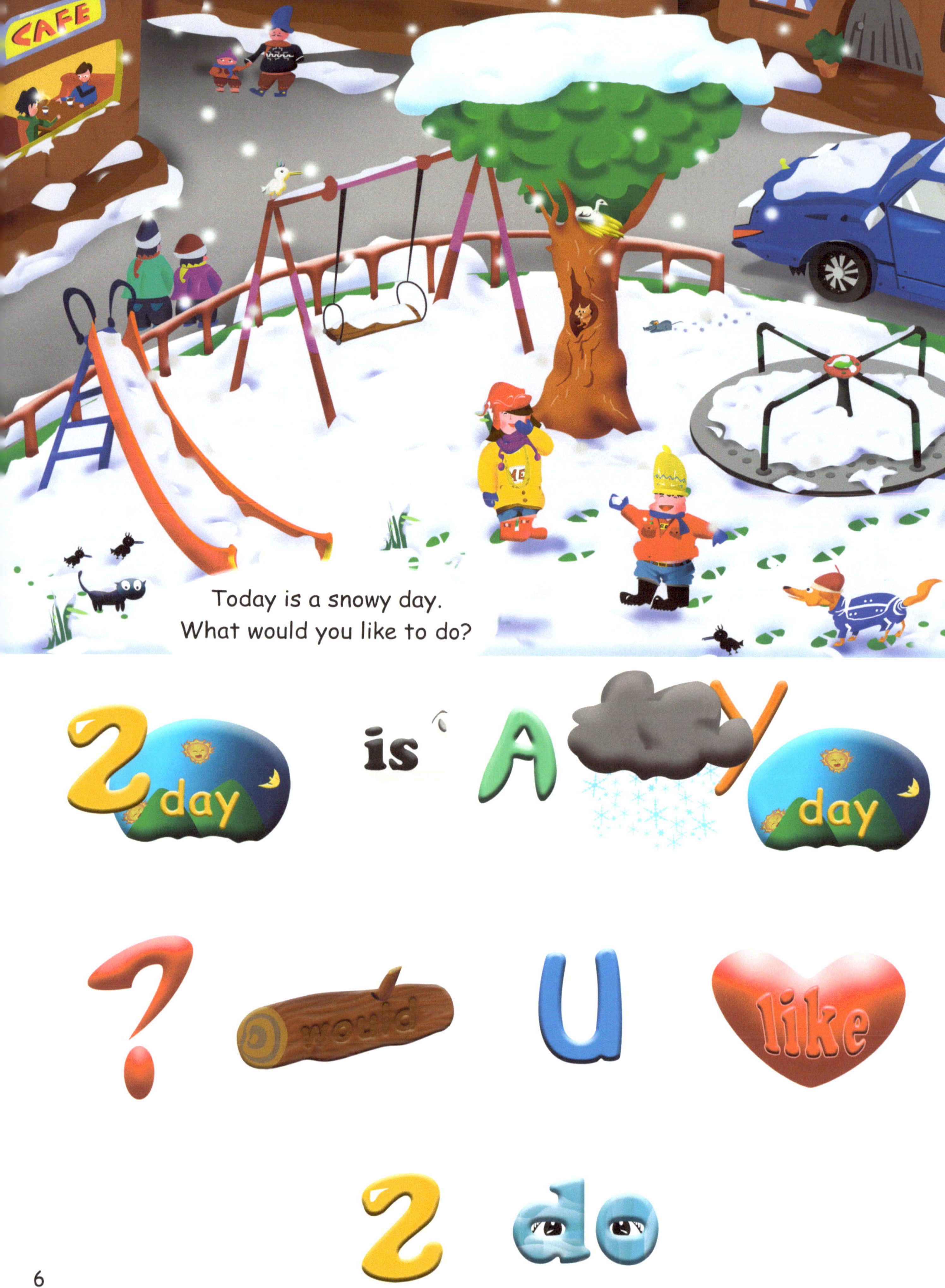

Today is a snowy day.
What would you like to do?
CAFE
2day is A snowy day
? would U like
2 do

I'd like to make
the world's biggest snowman.

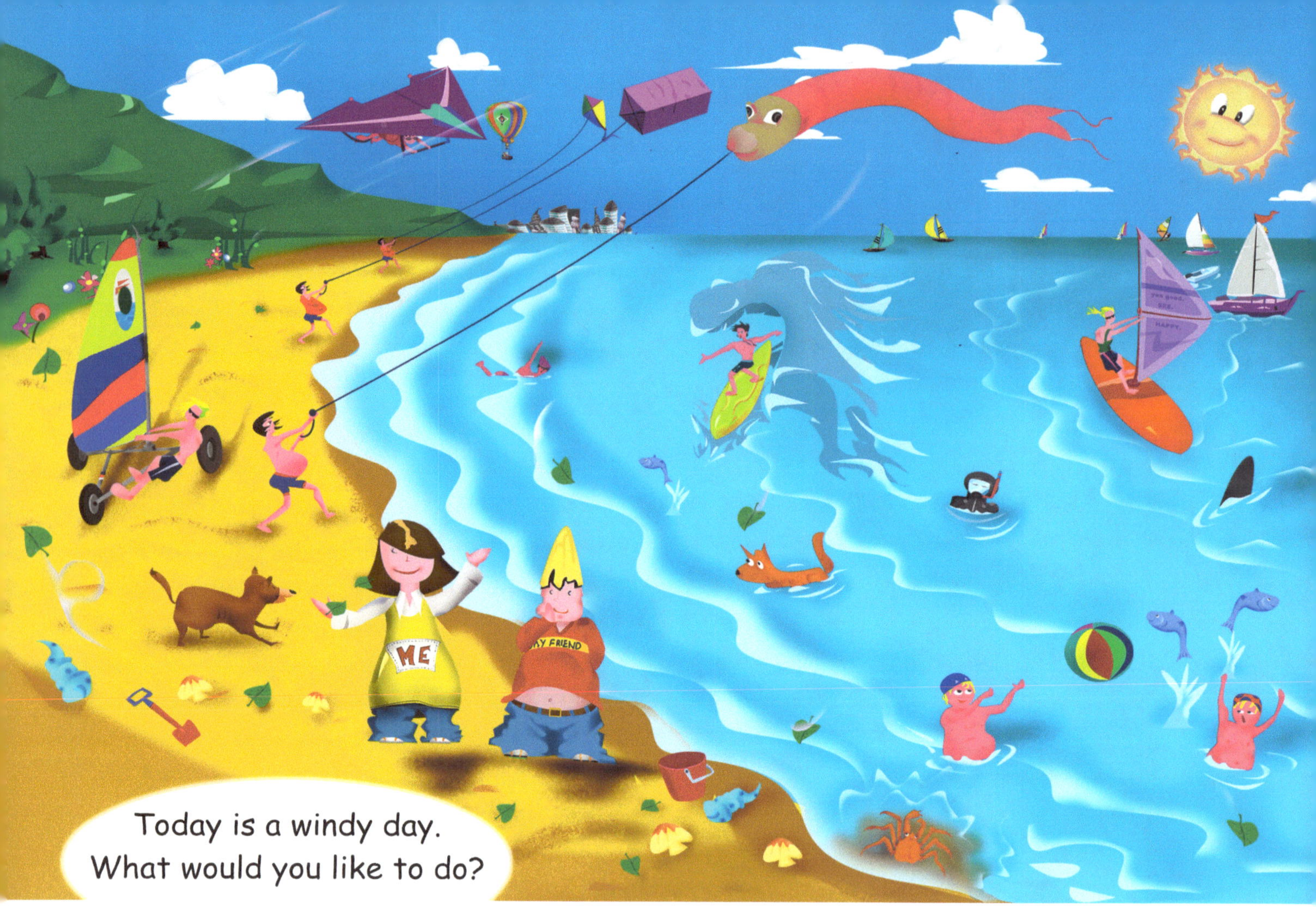

Today is a windy day.
What would you like to do?

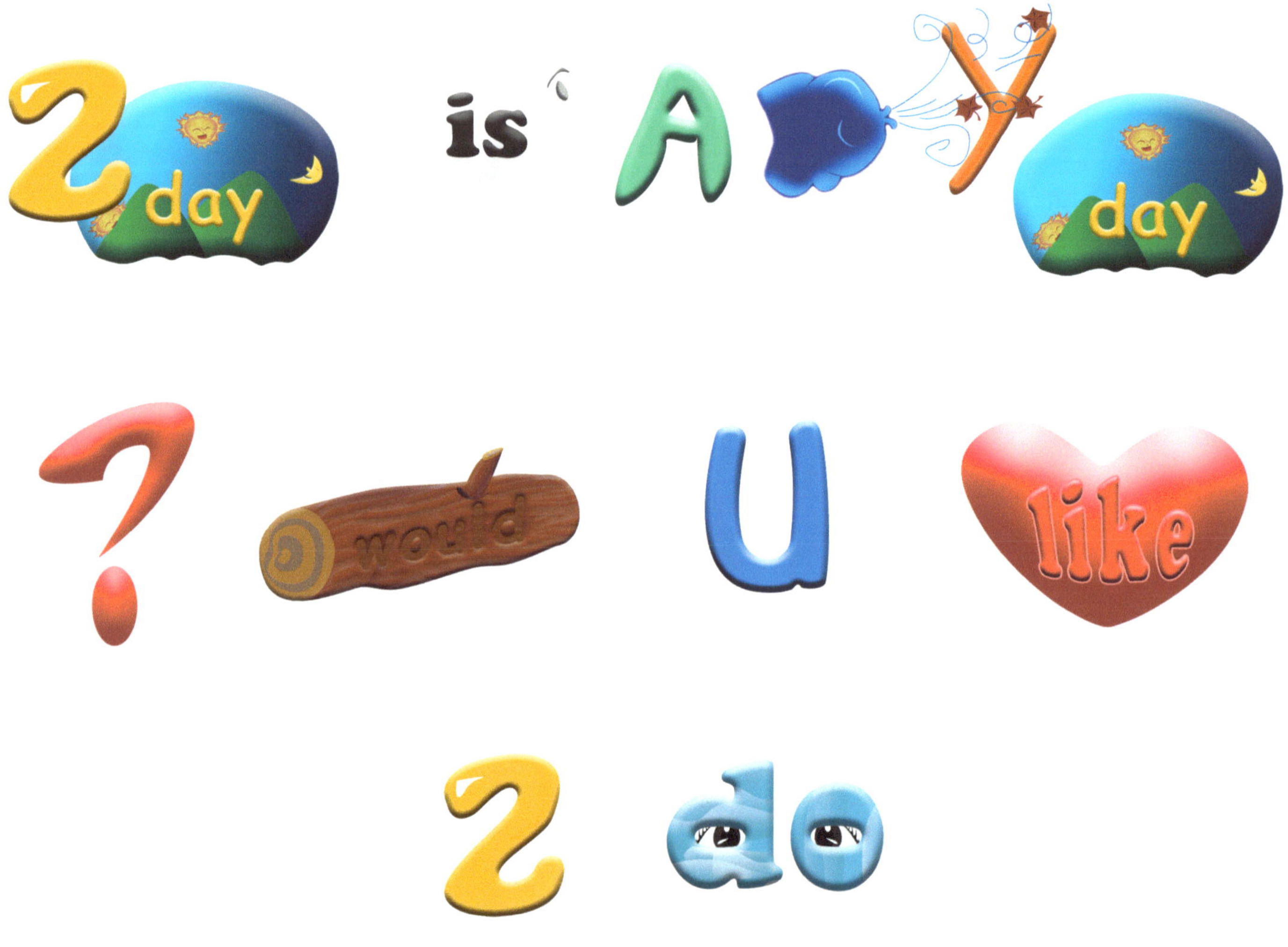

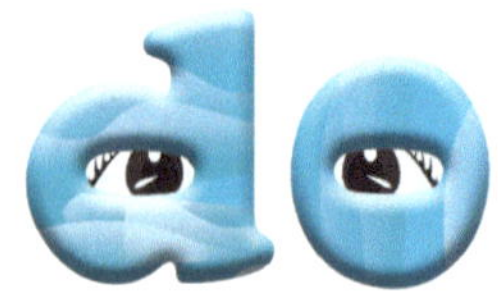

fast cat
MY FRIEND
KE
I'd like to sail
the world's fastest boat.
d
like
2
the
's
est

What's that?

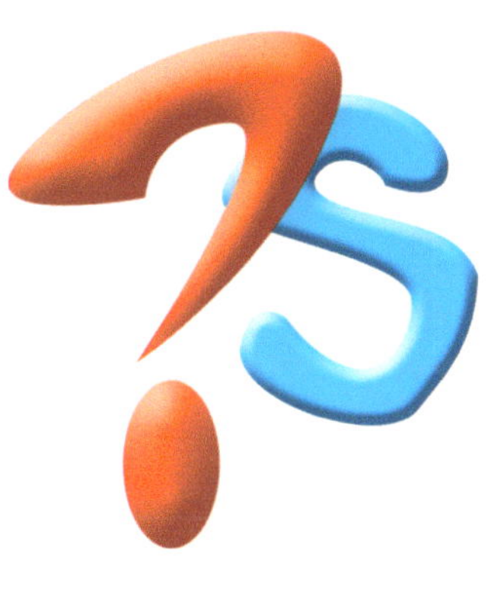

What's that?
And how do we
get there?
MY FRIEND
ME

MY FRIEND

ME

do

WE

get

It's Everest

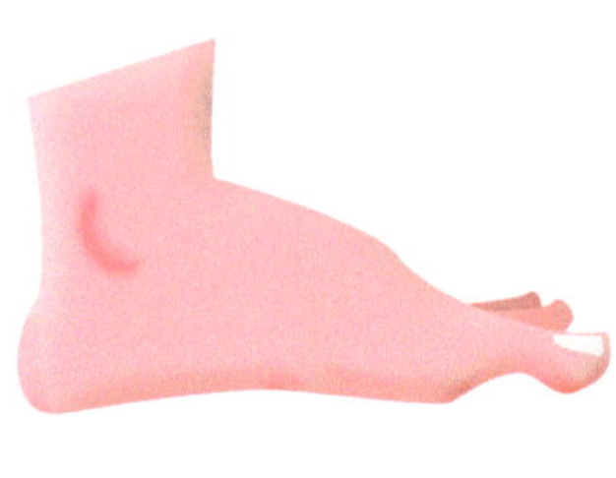

Let's go by
hot air balloon.
It's Ayers
rock.

It's
S
rock
ME
MY FRIEND
by
hot

It's the
Pyramids.
Let's go by camel.
It's the S
ME
by
MY FRIEND

It's the

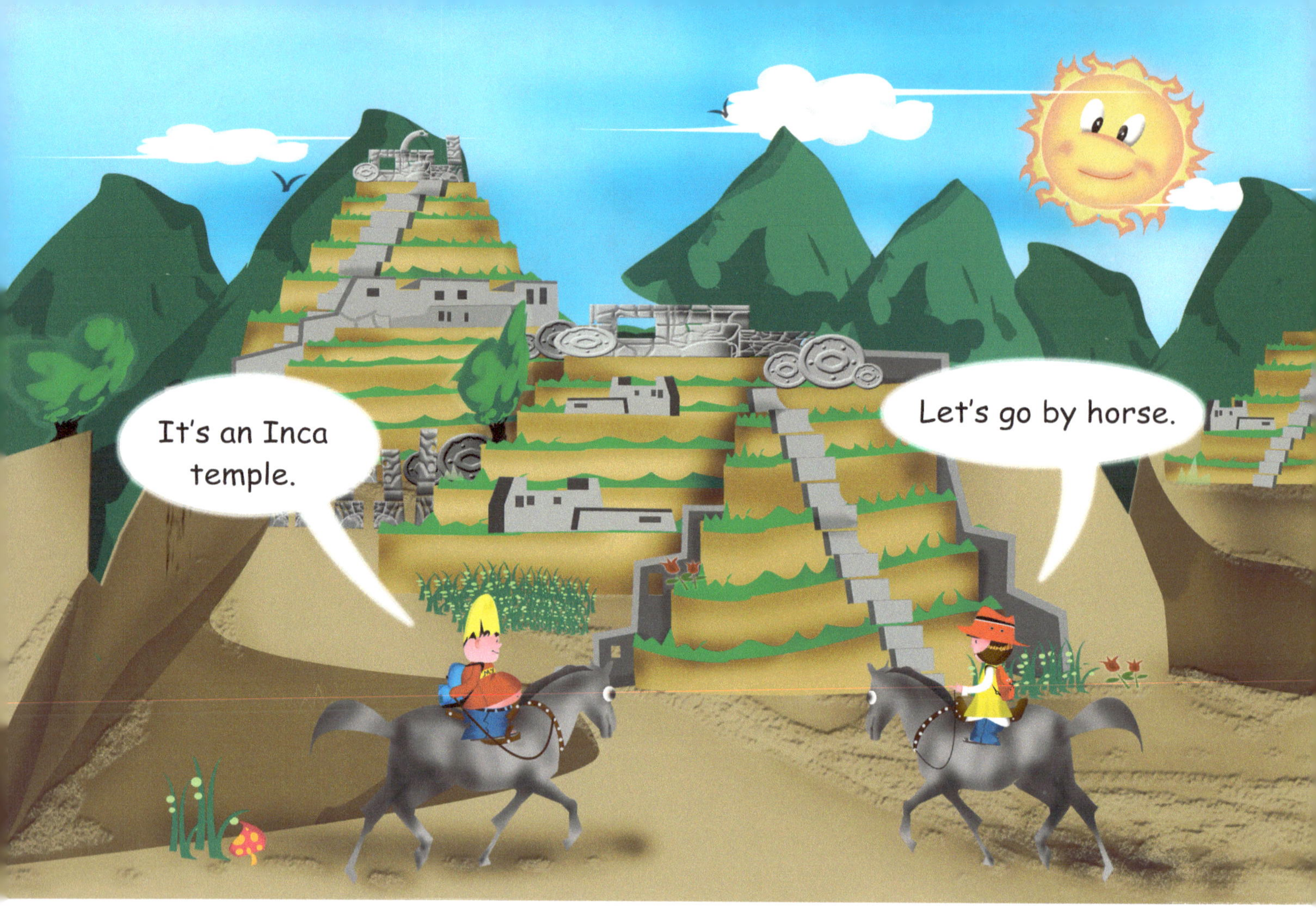

It's an  

It's Mount Rushmore.
Let's go by jeep.

It's

ME

by
MY FRIEND

It's a treasure
island.

Let's go by canoe.

It's A

ME

MY FRIEND

by

It's   the

Do you remember?

Pg 21   Do you remember the big, blue monster?

Pg 22   Yes, I remember. I remember the tall, green butterfly too.

Pg 23   Do you remember the school in the clouds?

Pg 24   Yes, I remember. I remember the slide around the tree too.

Pg 25   Do you remember the bath time machine?

Pg 26   Yes, I remember, and the boy playing in the mud.

Pg 27   All the things we can remember.

Pg 28   We can use at school this September.

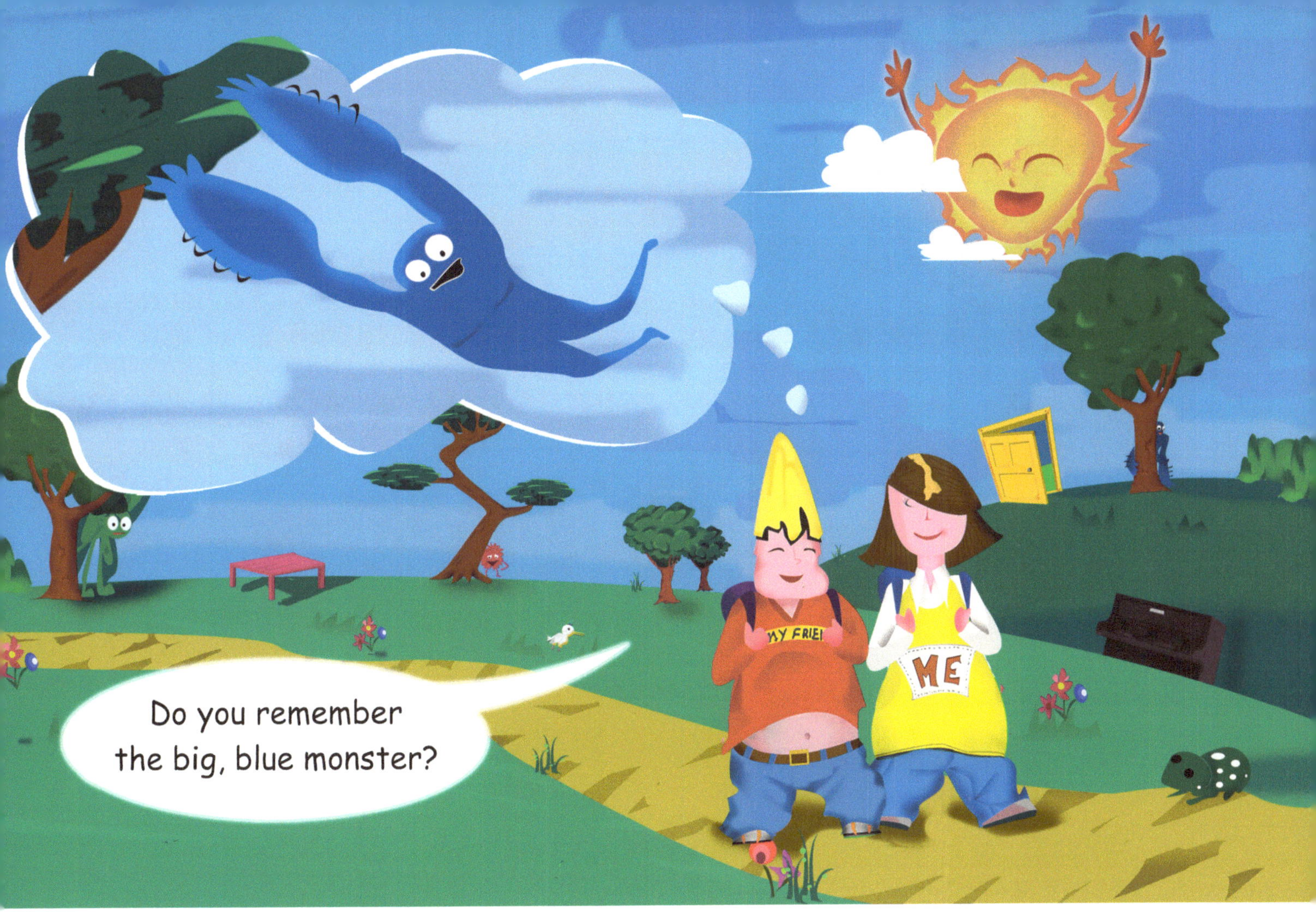

Do you remember
the big, blue monster?

do

U

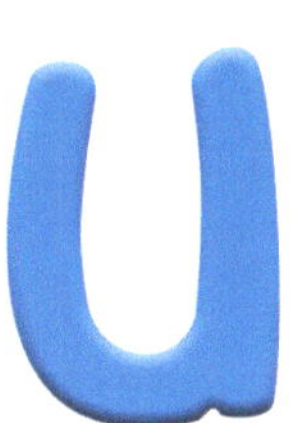

re
mem
ber

the

big
MY FRIEND

blue

Yes, I remember.
I remember the tall,
green butterfly too.

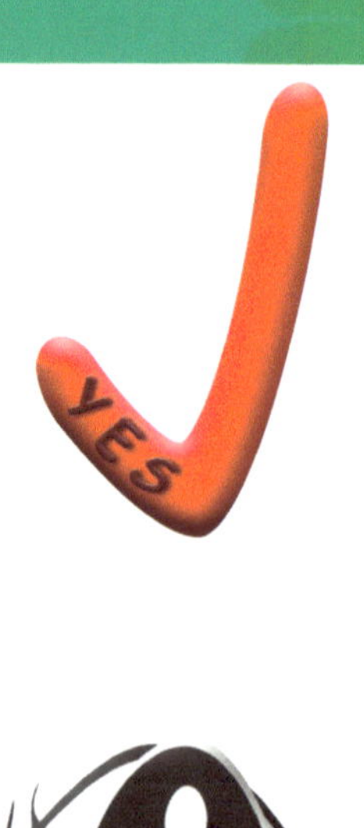

YES

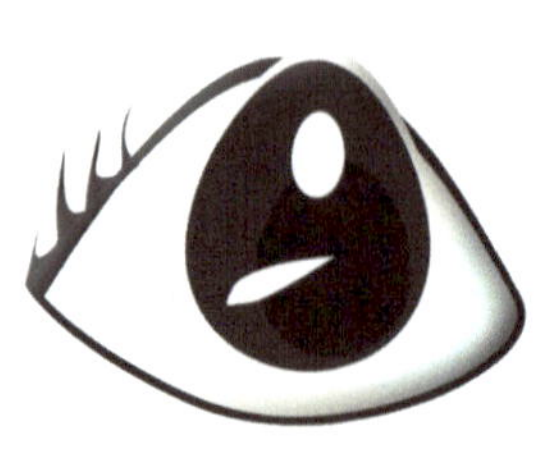

re mem ber

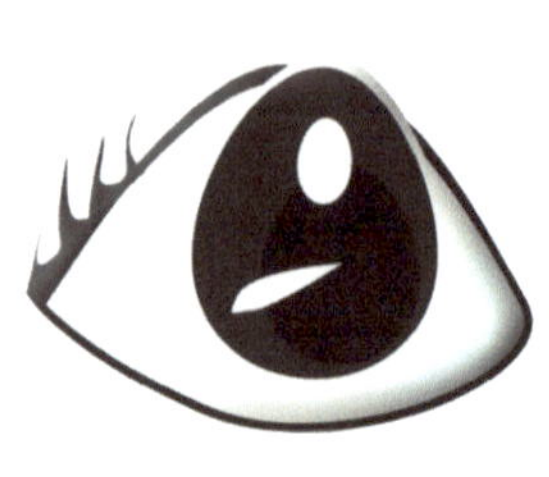

re mem ber

the

green

2

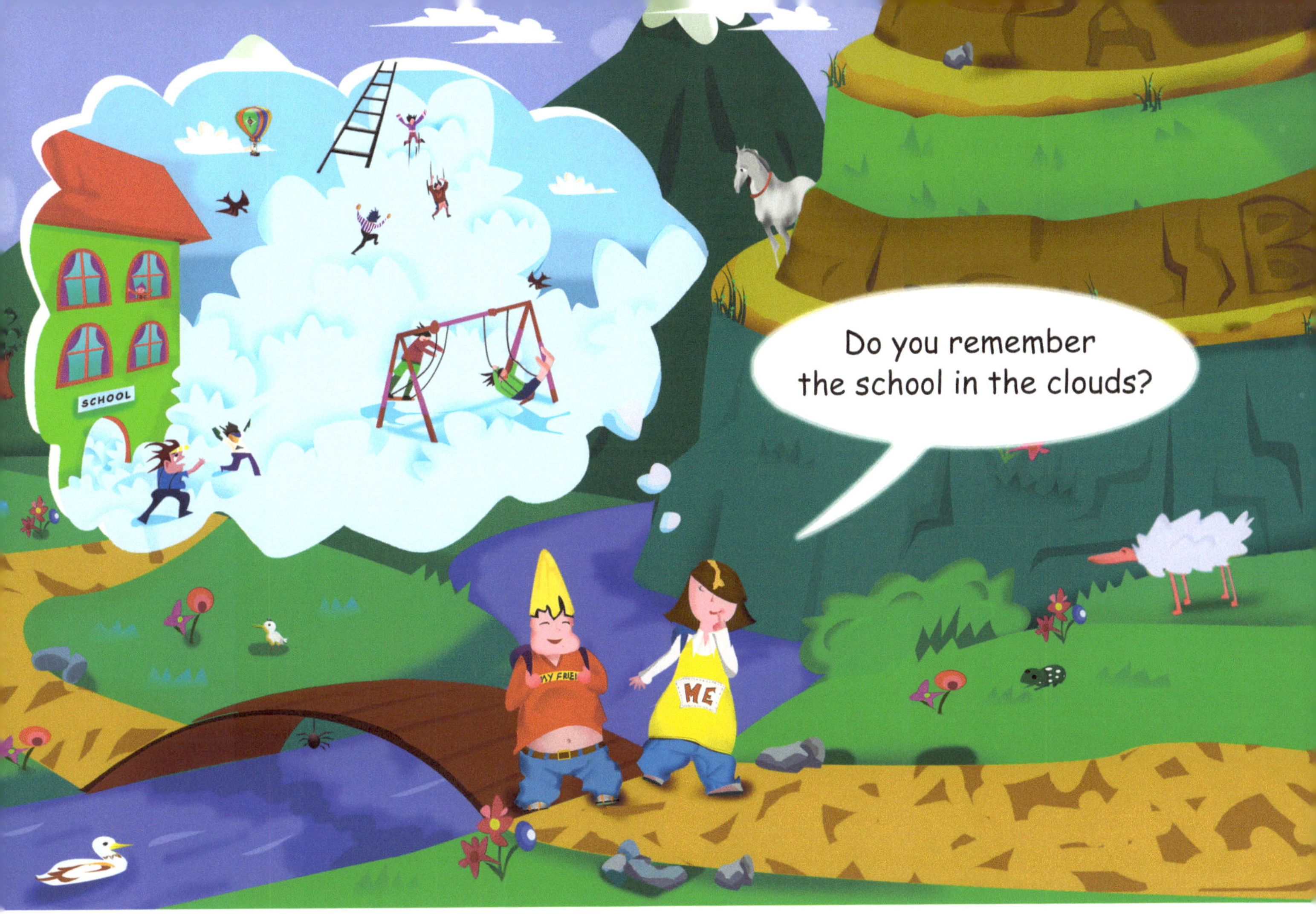

do U re mem ber

the

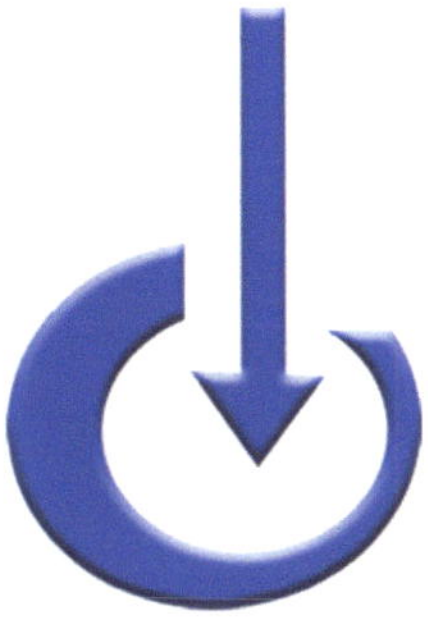

the

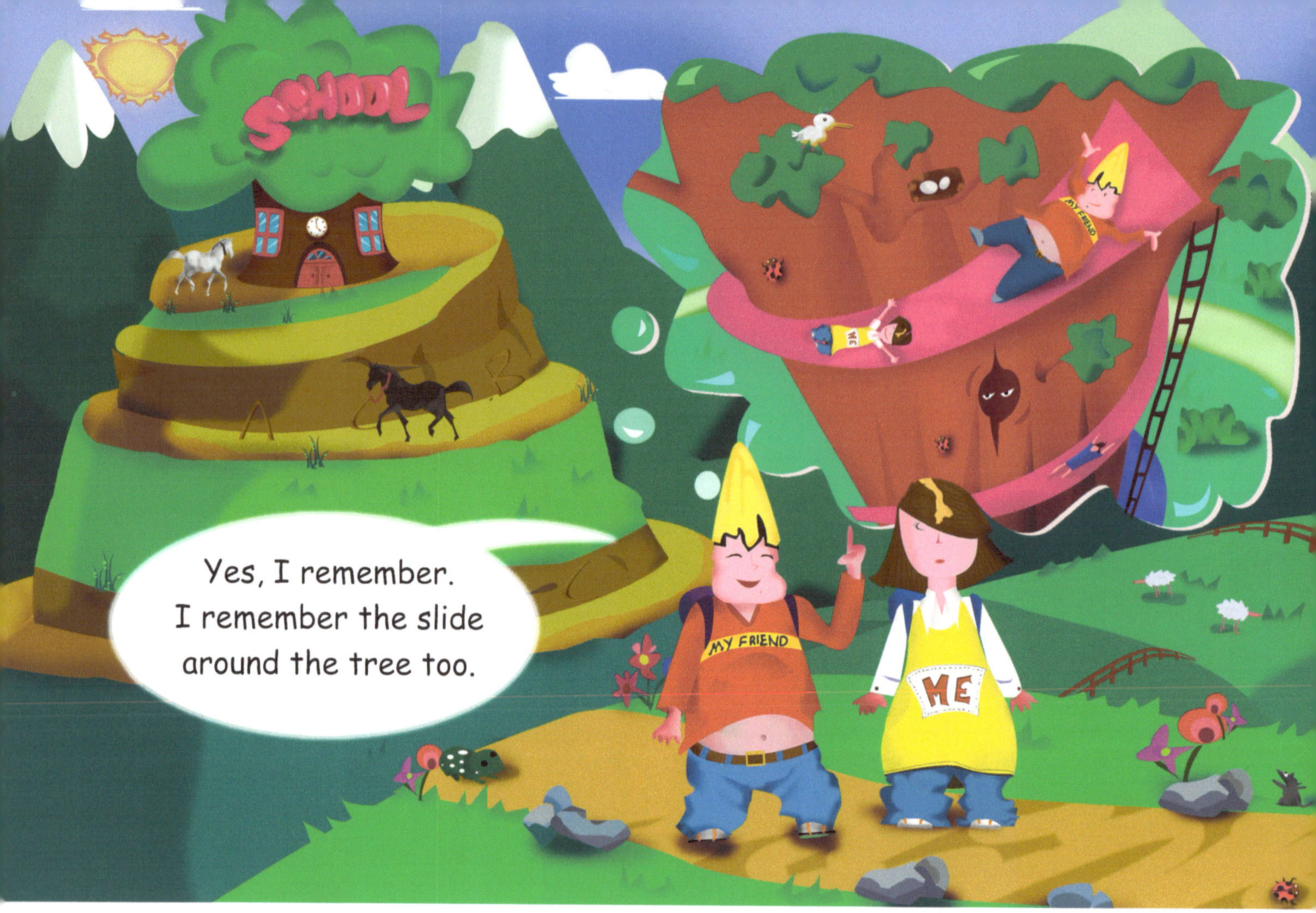

24

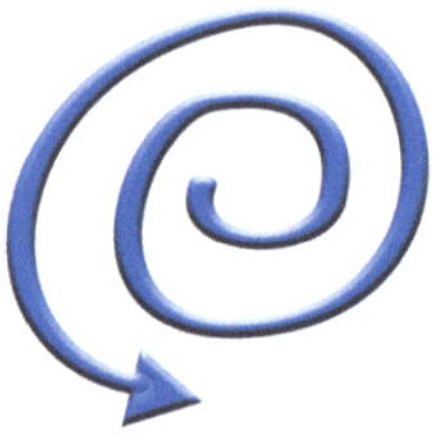

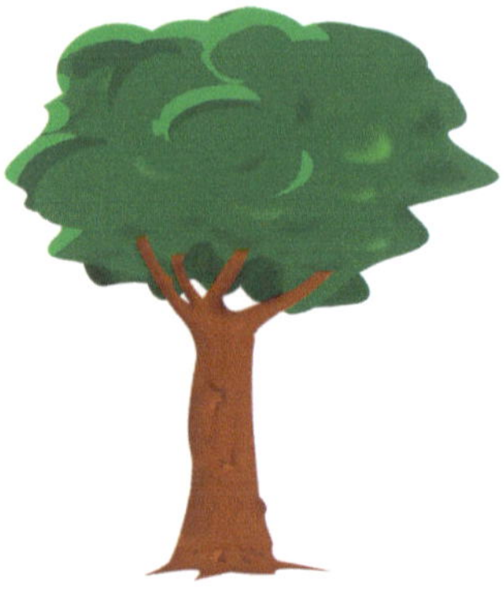

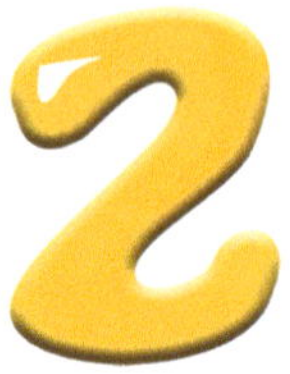

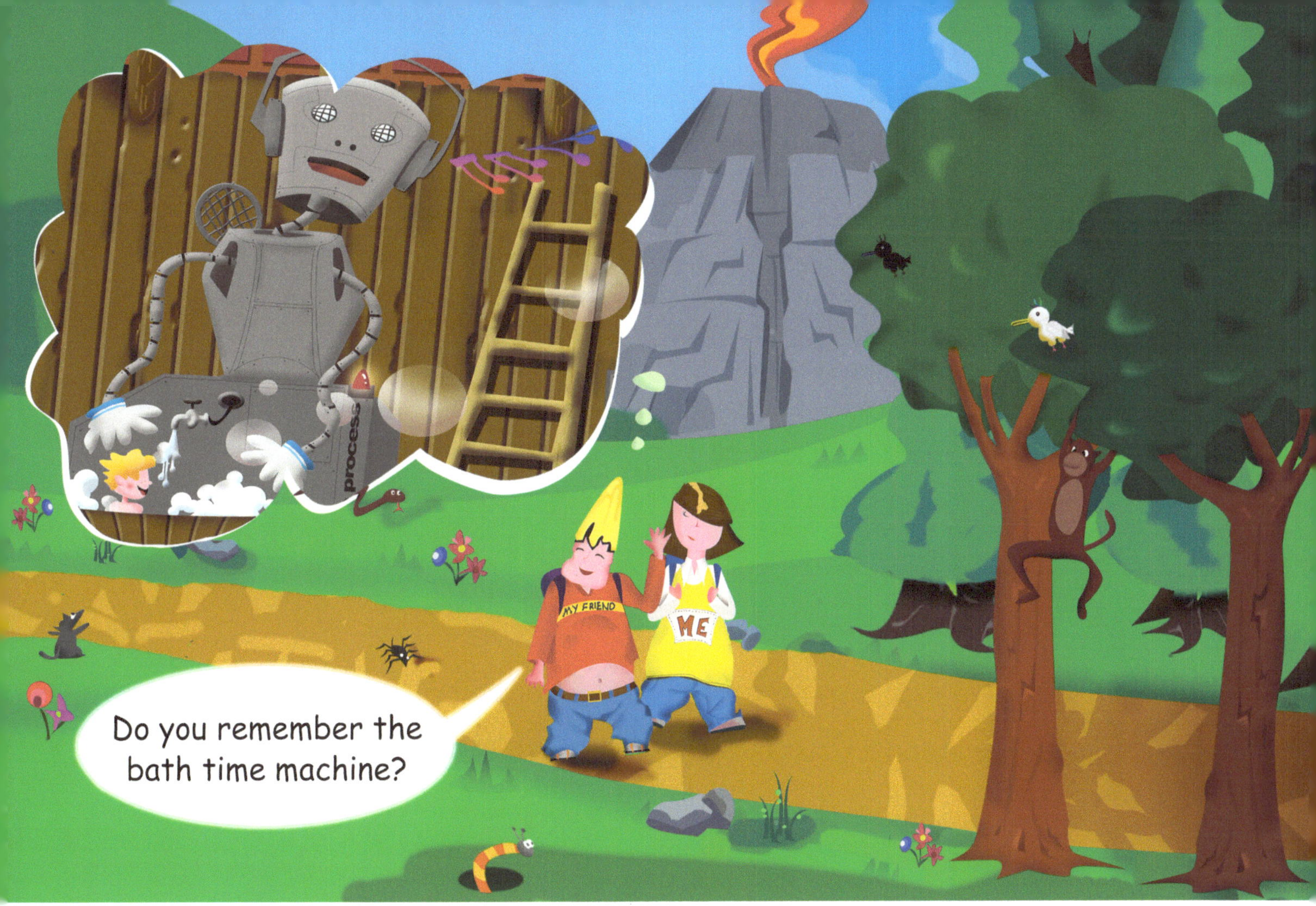

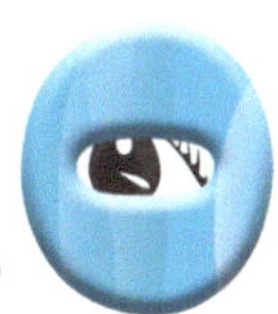

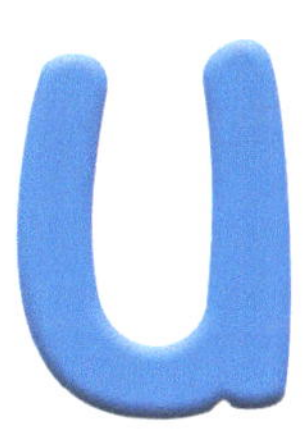

the

MY FRIEND
ME
Do you remember the
bath time machine?

do

U

re mem ber

Time

soap process

Yes, I remember.
And the boy playing
in the mud.

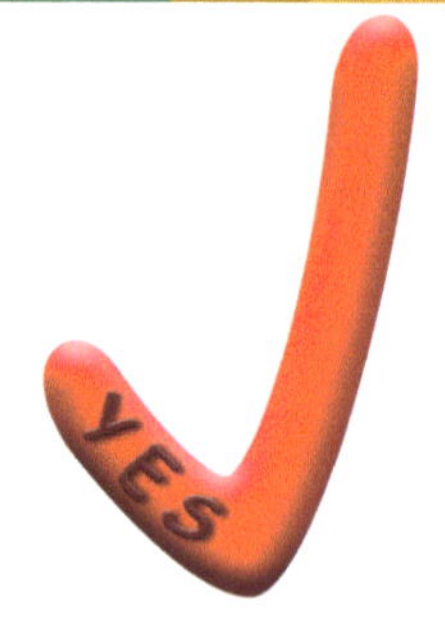
YES

re mem ber

the

ing

the

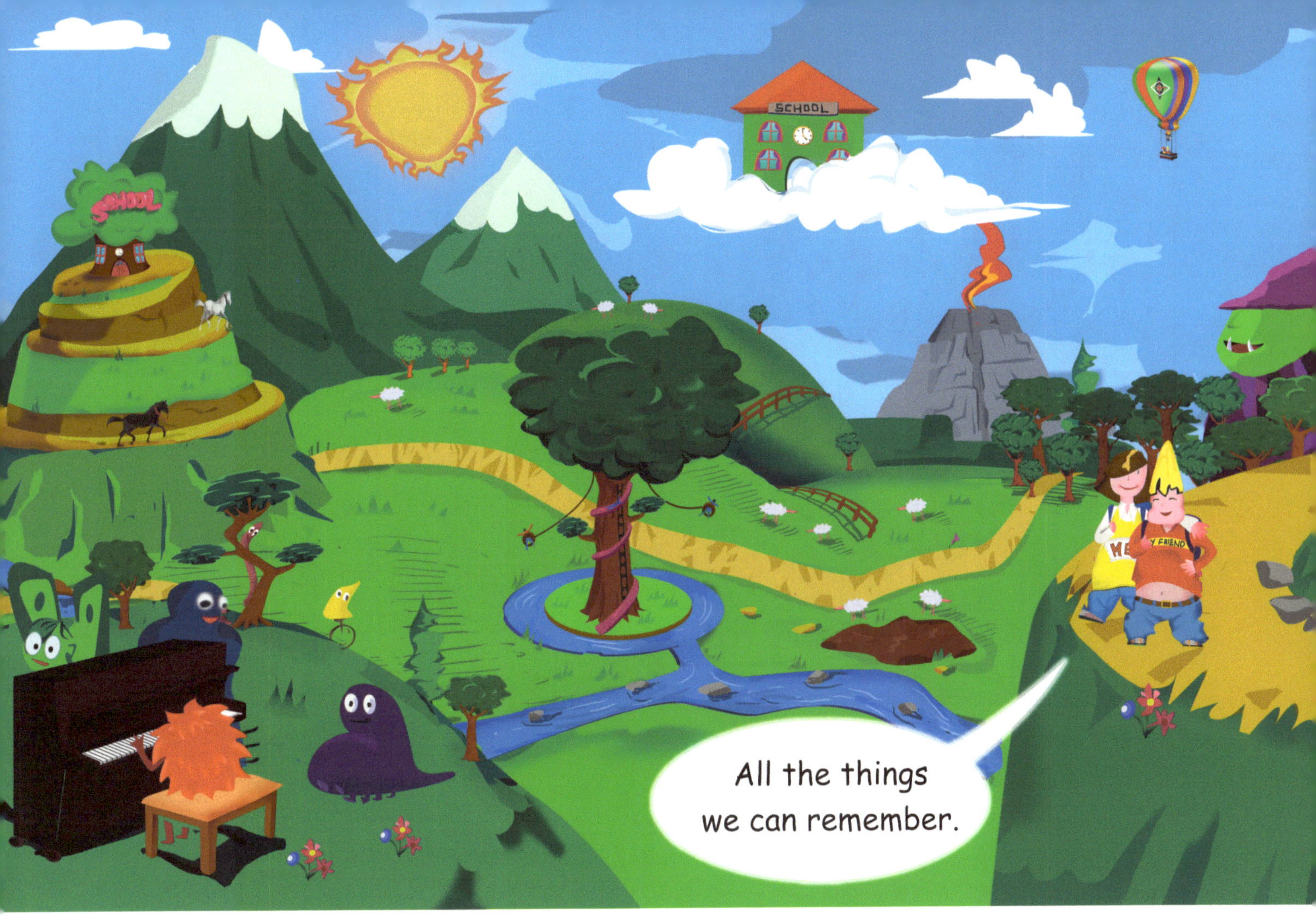
SCHOOL
SCHOOL
All the things
we can remember.

All
the
ME
WE
can
re
mem
ber

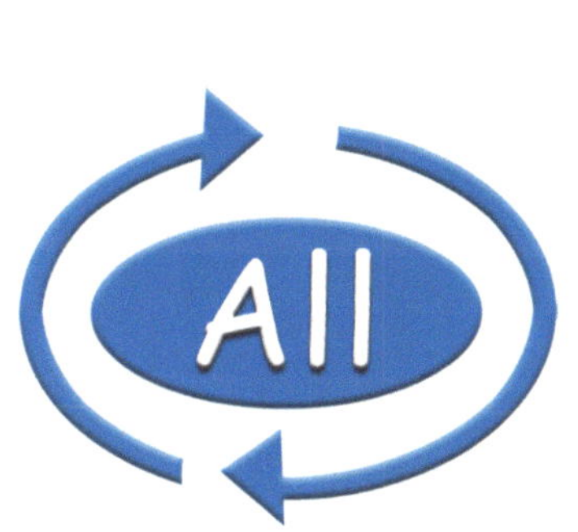

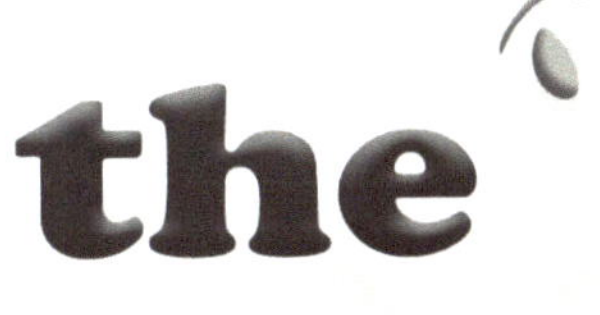

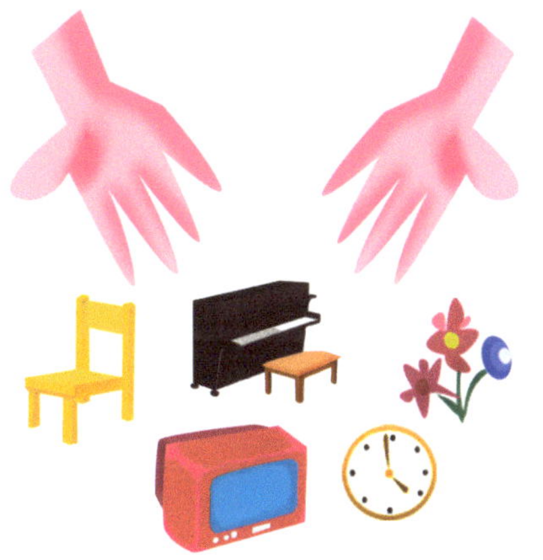

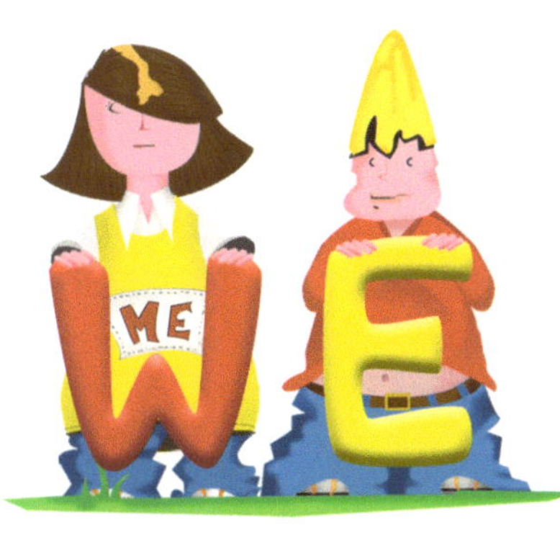

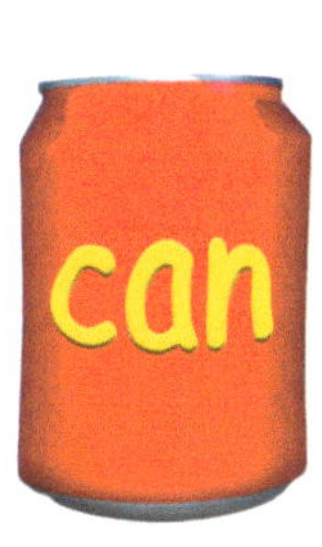

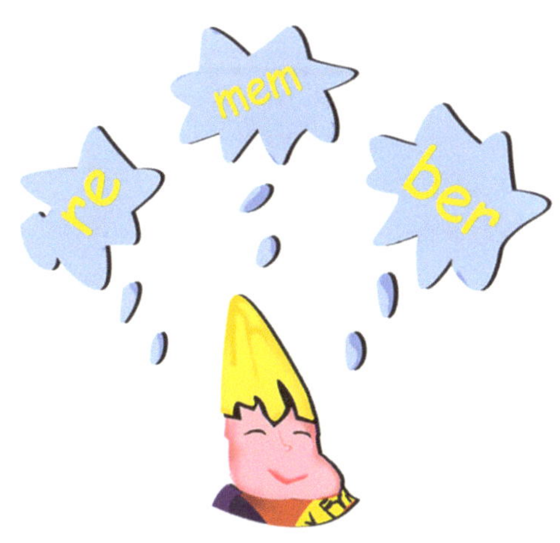

school
We can use in
school this September.

ME
WE
can
use
SCHOOL
September

Let's clean up

Have a good look at this street.
Let's clean up the litter
from what people eat.

Have   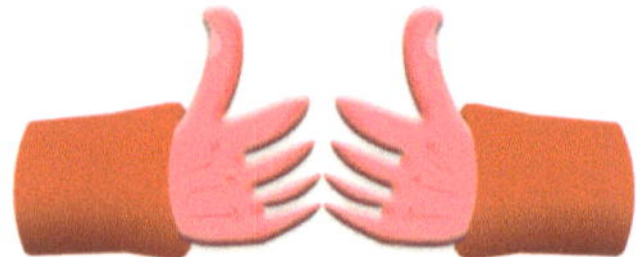

  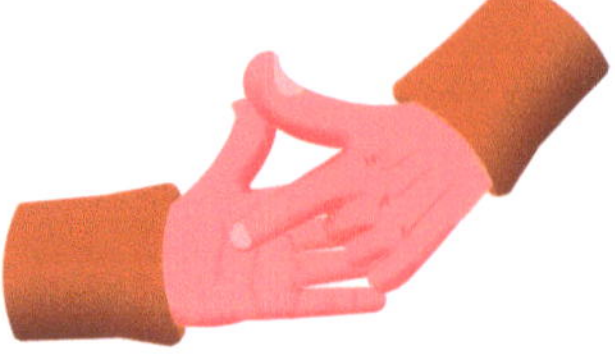

   **the** 

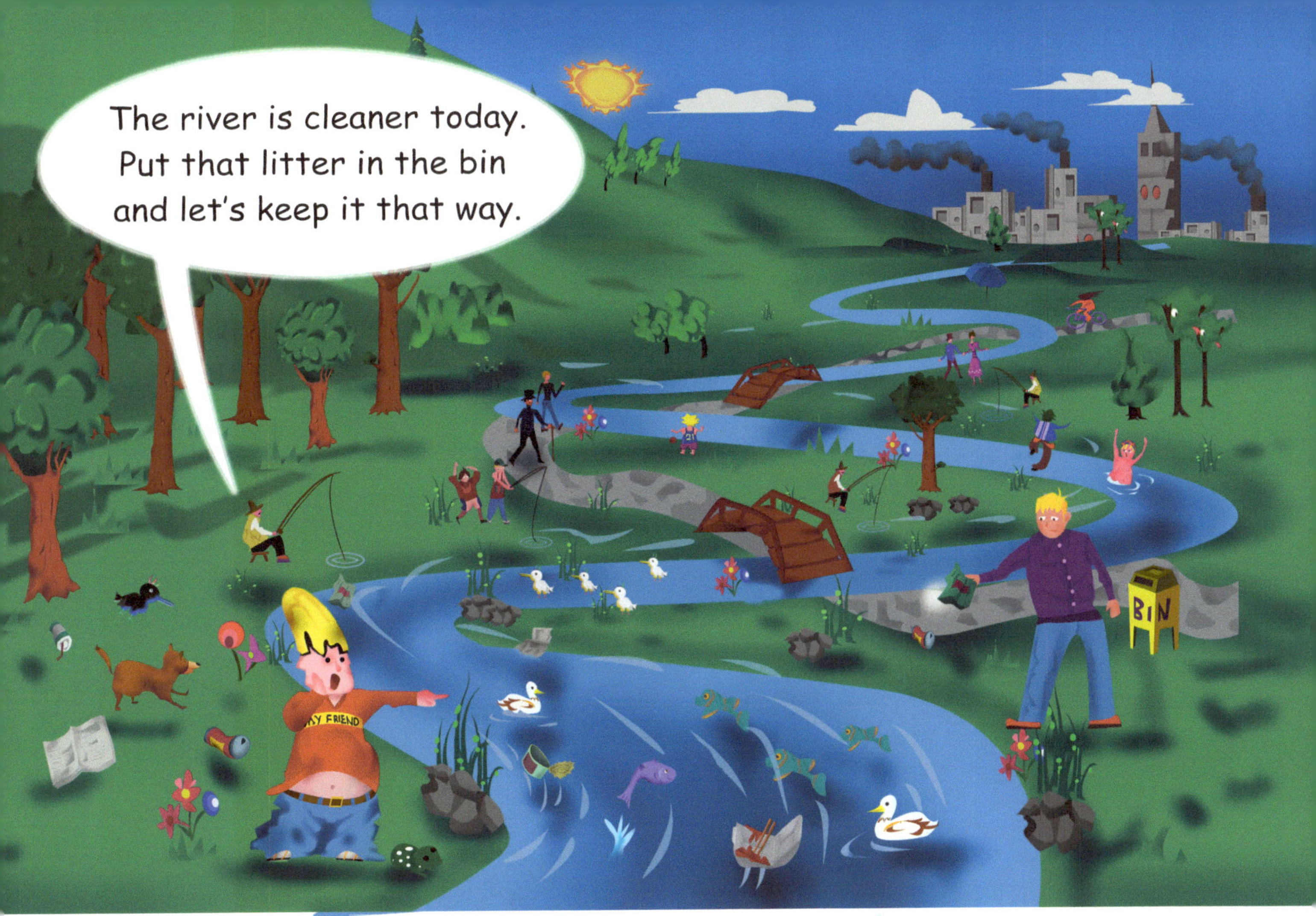

The river is cleaner today. Put that litter in the bin and let's keep it that way.

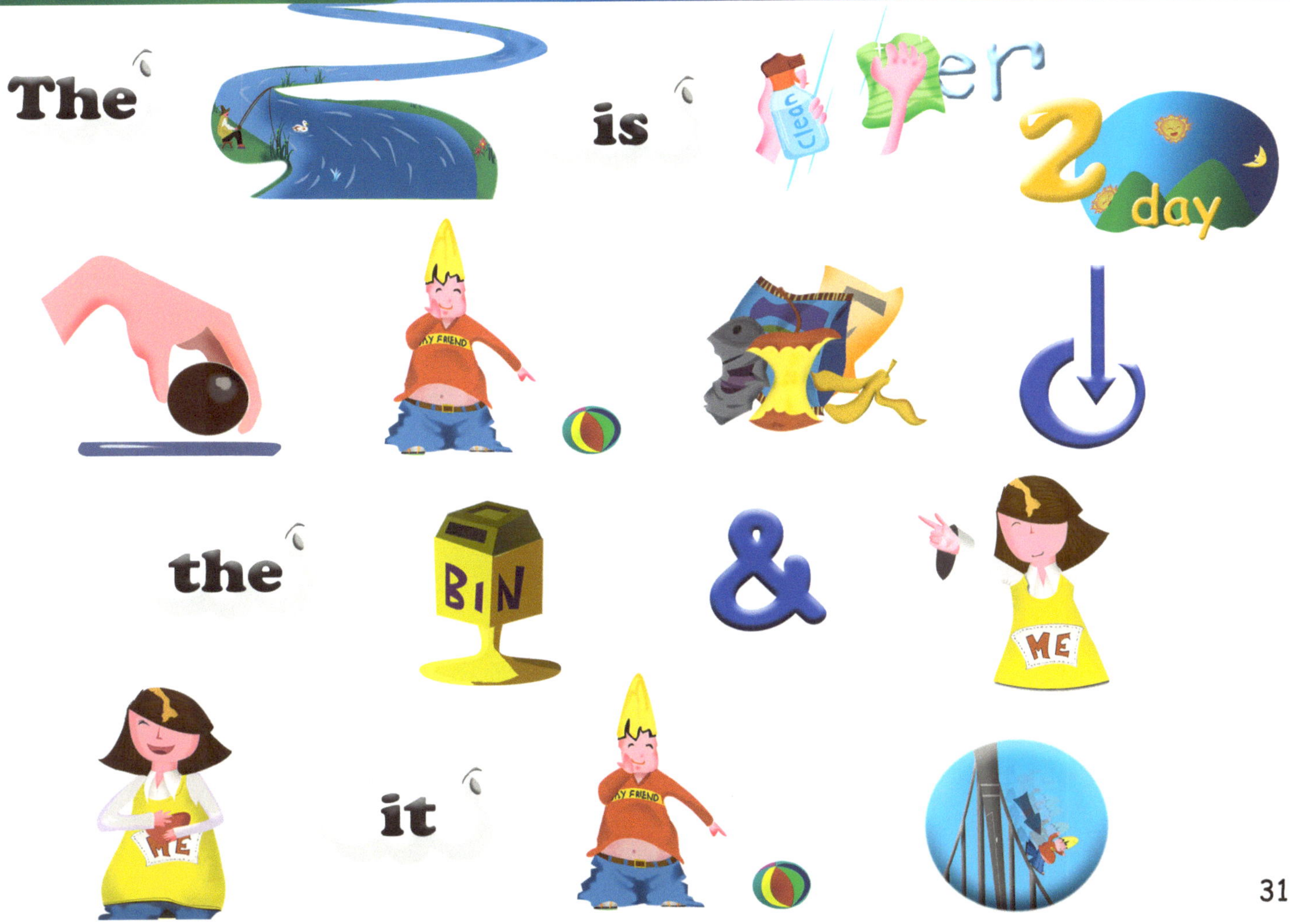

The
is
today
the
BIN
&
ME
it

the

the

the

At the beach we can swim in the sea.
Let's clean up the litter
so fish can swim free!

At the park there is so much to do.
First, let's clean up all that dog pooh.

the
PARK
is
so
2
do
1st
ME
Clean
all

If you'd like to show people you care,
stop throwing all your litter in the air.
If u'd like 2 show
u
stop ing all y?
the

Look! We can make our city
as clean as can be.

as  

 as 

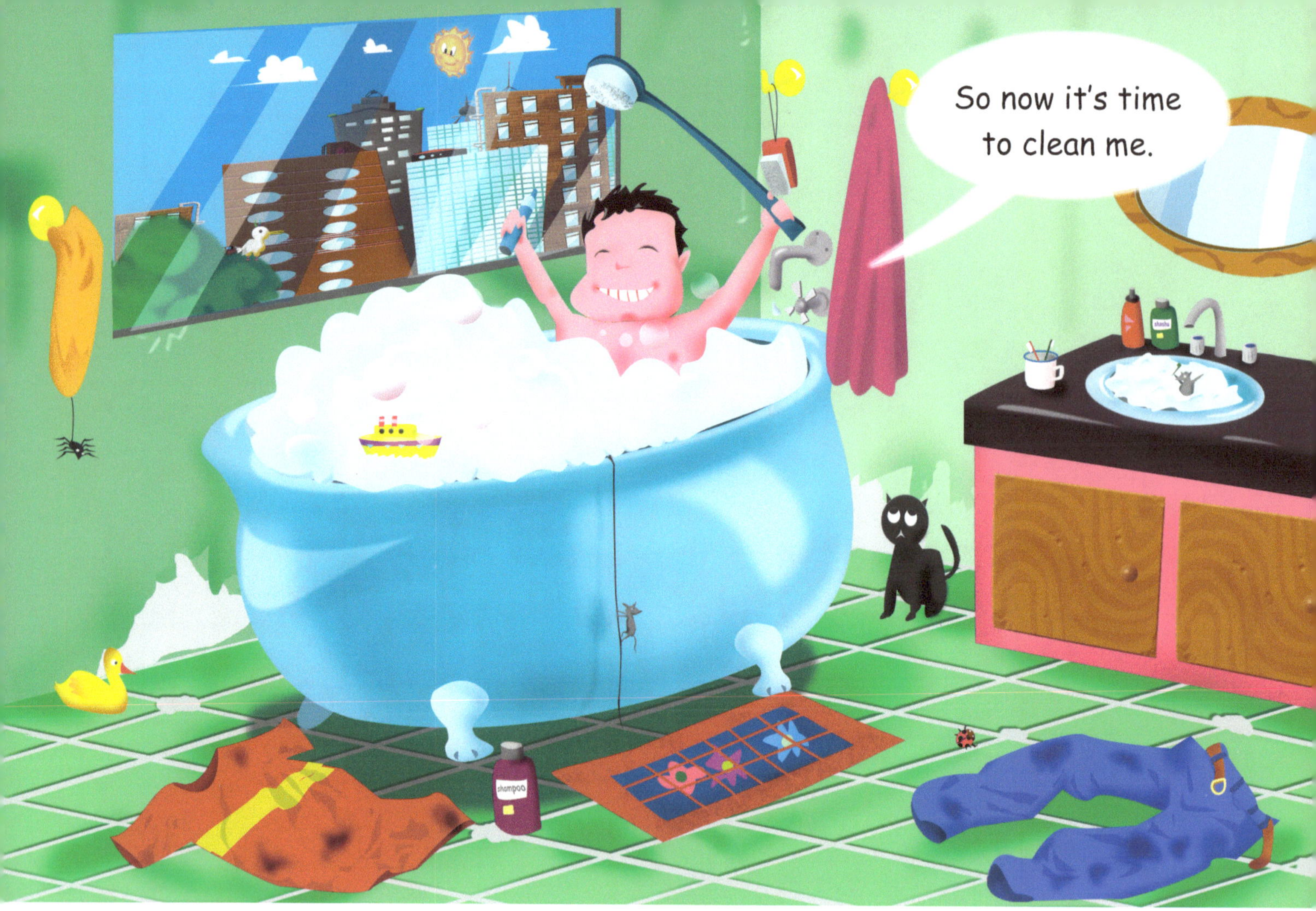

So now it's time
to clean me.

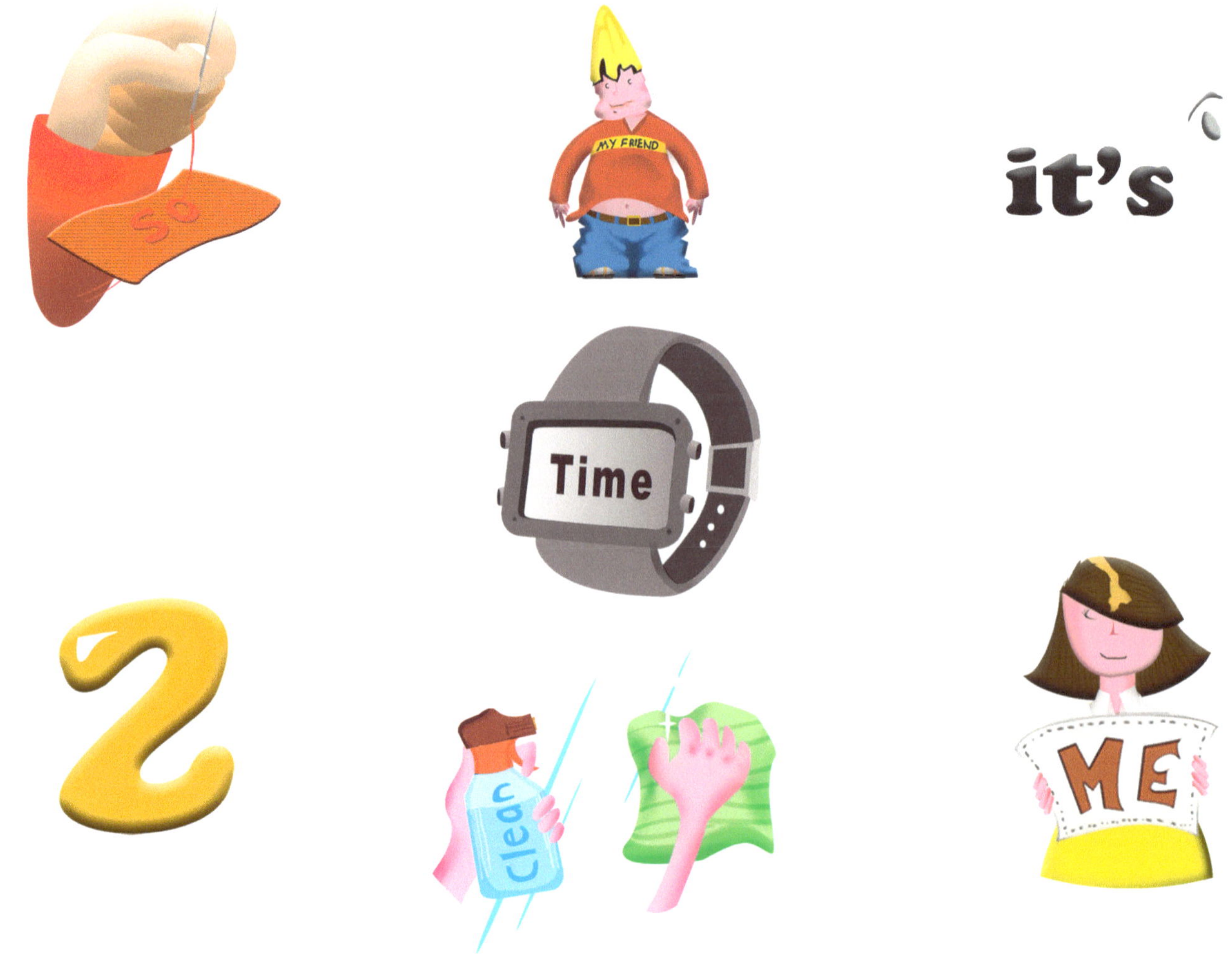

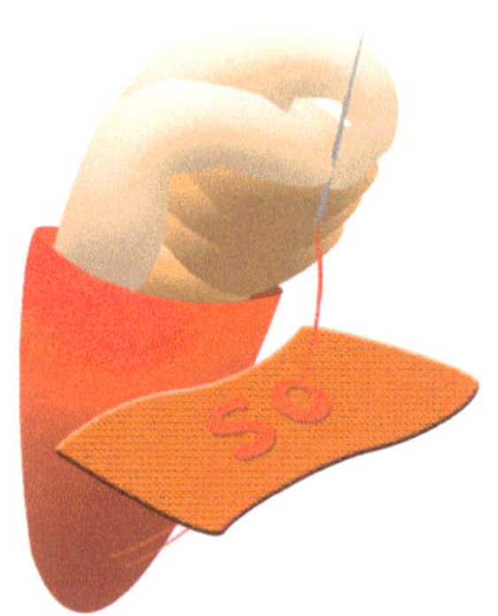

SO

MY FRIEND

it's

Time

clean

ME

Vocabulary

<table>
<tr><td>A</td><td>a</td><td>(art)</td></tr>
<tr><td></td><td>air</td><td>(n)</td></tr>
<tr><td></td><td>all</td><td>(adj)</td></tr>
<tr><td></td><td>also</td><td>(adv)</td></tr>
<tr><td></td><td>and</td><td>(conj)</td></tr>
<tr><td></td><td>any</td><td>(indef pron)</td></tr>
<tr><td></td><td>around</td><td>(adv)</td></tr>
<tr><td></td><td>at</td><td>(prep)</td></tr>
<tr><td></td><td>Ayers Rock</td><td>(n)</td></tr>
<tr><td>B</td><td>balloon</td><td>(n)</td></tr>
<tr><td></td><td>beach</td><td>(n)</td></tr>
<tr><td></td><td>beautiful</td><td>(adj)</td></tr>
<tr><td></td><td>better</td><td>(adj)</td></tr>
<tr><td></td><td>big</td><td>(adj)</td></tr>
<tr><td></td><td>bin</td><td>(n)</td></tr>
<tr><td></td><td>blue</td><td>(adj)</td></tr>
<tr><td></td><td>boat</td><td>(n)</td></tr>
<tr><td></td><td>butterfly</td><td>(n)</td></tr>
<tr><td></td><td>by</td><td>(prep)</td></tr>
<tr><td>C</td><td>camel</td><td>(n)</td></tr>
<tr><td></td><td>can</td><td>(n)</td></tr>
<tr><td></td><td>canoe</td><td>(modal v)</td></tr>
<tr><td></td><td>care</td><td>(v)</td></tr>
<tr><td></td><td>city</td><td>(n)</td></tr>
<tr><td></td><td>cloud</td><td>(n)</td></tr>
<tr><td></td><td>cool</td><td>(adj)</td></tr>
<tr><td>D</td><td>day</td><td>(n)</td></tr>
<tr><td></td><td>do</td><td>(vt.vi.)</td></tr>
<tr><td></td><td>dog</td><td>(n)</td></tr>
<tr><td></td><td>don't</td><td>(v) =do not</td></tr>
<tr><td></td><td>down</td><td>(adv part)</td></tr>
<tr><td></td><td>dinner</td><td>(n)</td></tr>
<tr><td></td><td>DJ</td><td>(n)</td></tr>
<tr><td></td><td>drink</td><td>(n)</td></tr>
<tr><td>E</td><td>eat</td><td>(vi.vt.)</td></tr>
<tr><td>F</td><td>fast</td><td>(adj)</td></tr>
<tr><td></td><td>favorite</td><td>(adj)</td></tr>
<tr><td></td><td>first</td><td>(adv)</td></tr>
<tr><td></td><td>fish</td><td>(n)</td></tr>
<tr><td></td><td>foot</td><td>(n)</td></tr>
<tr><td></td><td>free</td><td>(adj)</td></tr>
<tr><td></td><td>from</td><td>(prep)</td></tr>
<tr><td>G</td><td>get</td><td>(v)</td></tr>
<tr><td></td><td>go</td><td>(adj)</td></tr>
<tr><td></td><td>good</td><td>(v)</td></tr>
<tr><td></td><td>green</td><td>(adj)</td></tr>
<tr><td>H</td><td>happy</td><td>(adj)</td></tr>
<tr><td></td><td>have</td><td>(vt)</td></tr>
<tr><td></td><td>horse</td><td>(n)</td></tr>
<tr><td></td><td>hot</td><td>(adj)</td></tr>
<tr><td></td><td>how</td><td>(adv)</td></tr>
<tr><td>I</td><td>I</td><td>(pers pron)</td></tr>
<tr><td></td><td>I'd</td><td>(v) I'd = I would,</td></tr>
<tr><td></td><td>if</td><td>(conj)</td></tr>
<tr><td></td><td>in</td><td>(prep)</td></tr>
<tr><td></td><td>Inca Temple</td><td>(n)</td></tr>
<tr><td></td><td>is</td><td>(v)</td></tr>
<tr><td></td><td>it</td><td>(pron)</td></tr>
<tr><td></td><td>it's</td><td>(v) = it is</td></tr>
<tr><td>J</td><td>jeep</td><td>(n)</td></tr>
<tr><td></td><td>just</td><td>(adv)</td></tr>
<tr><td>K</td><td>keep</td><td>(vi.vt.)</td></tr>
<tr><td>L</td><td>let's</td><td>(v) = let us</td></tr>
<tr><td></td><td>like</td><td>(v)</td></tr>
<tr><td></td><td>litter</td><td>(n)</td></tr>
<tr><td></td><td>live</td><td>(v)</td></tr>
<tr><td></td><td>long</td><td>(adj)</td></tr>
<tr><td></td><td>look</td><td>(vi.vt.)</td></tr>
<tr><td>M</td><td>machine</td><td>(n)</td></tr>
<tr><td></td><td>make</td><td>(vt.vi)</td></tr>
<tr><td></td><td>marvelous</td><td>(adj)</td></tr>
<tr><td></td><td>mat</td><td>(n)</td></tr>
<tr><td></td><td>me</td><td>(pers pron)</td></tr>
<tr><td></td><td>monster</td><td>(n)</td></tr>
<tr><td></td><td>moon</td><td>(n)</td></tr>
<tr><td></td><td>Mount Everest</td><td>(n)</td></tr>
<tr><td></td><td>Mount Rushmore</td><td>(n)</td></tr>
<tr><td></td><td>much</td><td>(n)</td></tr>
<tr><td></td><td>mud</td><td>(n)</td></tr>
<tr><td></td><td>my</td><td>(poss)</td></tr>
<tr><td>N</td><td>now</td><td>(adv)</td></tr>
<tr><td>O</td><td>on</td><td>(adv part)</td></tr>
<tr><td></td><td>our</td><td>(adj)</td></tr>
<tr><td></td><td>out</td><td>(adv part)</td></tr>
<tr><td>P</td><td>park</td><td>(n)</td></tr>
<tr><td></td><td>people</td><td>(n)</td></tr>
<tr><td></td><td>please</td><td>(int)</td></tr>
<tr><td></td><td>pooh</td><td>(int)</td></tr>
<tr><td></td><td>primary</td><td>(adj)</td></tr>
<tr><td></td><td>put</td><td>(vi.vt.)</td></tr>
<tr><td></td><td>pyramids</td><td>(n)</td></tr>
<tr><td>Q</td><td>quiet</td><td>(adj)</td></tr>
<tr><td>R</td><td>rainy</td><td>(adj)</td></tr>
<tr><td></td><td>remember</td><td>(vi.vt.)</td></tr>
<tr><td></td><td>river</td><td>(n)</td></tr>
<tr><td></td><td>rocket</td><td>(n)</td></tr>
</table>

Vocabulary

S	sail	(v)
	sea	(n)
	show	(vt.vi.)
	slide	(v)
	snowman	(n)
	snowy	(adj)
	so	(adv)
	start	(vt.vi.)
	street	(n)
	submarine	(n)
	sunny	(adj)
	swim	(vt.vi.)
T	that	(pron)
	the	(adv)
	there	(adv)
	this	(pron)
	throw	(vt.vi.)
	time	(n)
	Titanic	(n)
	to	(prep)
	today	(adv)
	Treasure Island	(n)
U	up	(adv)
	use	(n)
V	vet	(n)
	view	(n)
	very	(adv)
W	want	(vt.vi.)
	way	(n)
	we	(pron)
	what	(adv)
	windy	(adj)
	world	(n)
	would	(aux)
Y	yes	(adv)
	you	(pron)

I'd Like Song

To-day is a sun-ny day, what would you
like to do? To-day is a sun-ny day, what would you
like to do? I'd like to slide down the world's long-est
slide. To-day is a sno-wy day, what would you

I'd Like Song

like to do? To-day is a sno-wy day, what would you
like to do? I'd like to make the world's big-gest snowman. To-day is a win-dy day, what would you
like to do? To-day is a win-dy day, what would you

I'd Like Song

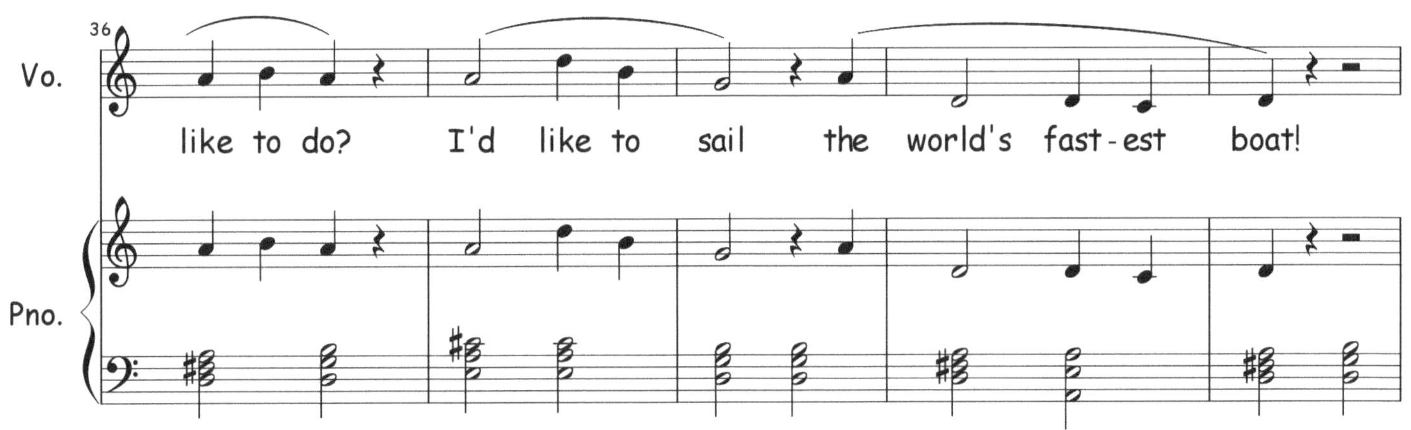

What's That Song

What's That Song
Vo. 1
Wait? Wait?
Let's go by ca-mel.
Vo. 2
Wait! Wait!
How do we get there?
Pno.
Hey, what's that?
It's the Ti-ta-nic?
It's the Ti-ta-nic.
Let's go!
Wait? Wait?
Let's go by
Yeah!
Wait! Wait!
How do we get there?
sub - ma - rine!
43

Do You Remember Song

Do You Remember Song

Let's Clean Up Song

Let's Clean Up Song

Let's Clean Up Song

Learn to Read with Images: An Introduction

Learn to Read with Images is a creative educational resource designed to make reading easier and more visually engaging. The philosophy is simple, effective, and suitable for learners of any age. This self-paced learning and teaching tool is highly convenient for use at home or in the classroom. It is targeted at beginner readers and is also beneficial to ESL and visual learners who struggle with literacy and breaking down phonics patterns.

Progressive Reading Levels

Learn to Read with Images is the key to unlocking each child's reading potential. There are six levels, each containing four stories that progressively increase in difficulty. Each level uses rhyme, sentence patterns, and elements of compound learning. The colorful, age-appropriate 'learning images' help early readers 'see' the words so they can connect the image to a word, and then easily decode (sound them out). By engaging more deeply with the content, readers can make quick connections, which aid significantly with vocabulary retention and memorization.

How Does *Learn to Read with Images* Work?

Learn to Read with Images is a simple, two-part learning process, as shown below.

- The upper half of each page tells a story and provides a visual environment for children to use their imagination.
- The bottom half of each page uses 'learning images' to represent the words in the story and helps with the pronunciation of more complex words.

Sight words that appear frequently are represented as 'text on a cloud' to help the students memorize words when it's time to read without the aid of the 'learning images.' This creative approach helps keep children interested so they can concentrate on learning vocabulary and fluency.

How Can You Use *Learn to Read with Images*?
It's as easy as 1-2-3!

1) As with any story, begin by reading to children, using the illustrations to help tell the story and spark their imagination.

2) Point to the 'learning images' as you pronounce each word. It is important that children learn to point to the words too, so urge them to point along with you as soon as possible. Help cement their recognition of the 'learning images' by repeatedly asking what it says.

3) Take time between pages to develop recognition of the 'learning images' by asking children to point at particular words and pronounce them. While they are not yet reading the written word, this is the first step in learning to read, which is exciting for everyone!

How Can Readers Build Confidence?

Begin with an easy 'learning image', like an eye. Keep in mind that 'learning images' are a visual tool to help make a connection between the image, its pronunciation, and the written form of the word. For example, the image of an eye is used to phonetically represent the word 'I', as well as 'eye', the actual word itself.

These regular prompts are important to ensure that children are learning to recognize the 'learning images' and not just memorizing words or sentences.

How Do You Know Readers Are Ready for the Next Level of *Learn to Read with Images*?

Once readers can correctly identify a word and its connection to the 'learning image', they are ready for the next level of *Learn to Read with Images*. There are several sight words in the text. For younger children, it is recommended to count the number of words in the text (upper half of the page) and do the same for the 'learning images' (bottom half of the page). This is a useful prompt to remind children that not all words in the text are connected to a 'learning image', and therefore, they must read from memory. As children move up the levels, they will recognize and strengthen their recognition of words, making them more fluent readers.